I WANT BE LIKE...

Combining Critical & Creative Thinking and Character Education

LOYALTY
COURAGE
HONESTY
PERSEVERANCE
COMMITMENT
GENEROSITY
RESPECT

Written by

Jim Mc Alpine   Sue Jeweler
Betty Weincek   Marion Finkbinder

Illustrated by Karen Neulinger

Educational Impressions™

ISBN 1-56644-958-8

© 1994 Educational Impressions, Inc., Hawthorne, NJ

Printed in the U.S.A.

EDUCATIONAL IMPRESSIONS, INC.
Hawthorne, NJ 07507

Table of Contents

Introduction

A recent Governors' Conference on Education stressed the need for problem solvers and ethical behaviors for the future of our society. To address these concerns and this issue in the school environment, we have written *I Want to Be Like*. The work provides students with biographical sketches of exemplary individuals as well as direct and implied instruction in creative problem solving, research skills, and analysis of the thinking process. Students arc also offered opportunities to transfer and apply ethical decision making to their own lives and the world in which they live.

What is a valuable human quality?
Courage?
Honesty?
Loyalty?
Generosity?
Perseverance?
Respect?
Commitment?
Yes.

Over time individuals model these qualities. As a result of their behaviors and influence on their society, they affect change on society itself.

By exploring and understanding the positive effect exemplary individuals have had on their societies, students will begin to appreciate these qualities. Once they understand the quality and its role in society, students may be able to perceive and emulate that quality in their own world.

In order for students to effectively use *I Want to Be Like,* they should be familiar with 1) the purpose and function of the each step of creative problem solving; 2) the purpose and function of each level of thinking according to Bloom's Taxonomy; and 3) the purpose and function of each step of the research scheme.

Once students have been introduced to these concepts, direct instruction should take place to demonstrate the purpose and value of integrating these concepts. Realizing the importance of the combination of these skills, students will then be able to apply the procedure to the given biographical information and the questions and activities presented in this text.

Successful experiences with *I Want to Be Like* will encourage and enable students to transfer the integration of creative problem solving, thinking skills and research skills to other situations far beyond the scope of this book.

NOTE: The information needed to research the material in this workbook is readily available in encyclopedias and in trade books found in most school and public libraries.

GOALS

I Want to Be Like is designed to...

1. give students the opportunity to think analytically

2. introduce students to historical or contemporary figures who exemplify specific qualities, values or characteristics which this society has identified as desirable and to examine the impact these have/are having on society

3. provide students with the opportunity to make comparative analyses of real historical or contemporary individuals who could be identified as exemplary models

4. provide students with the opportunity to analyze literary figures who could be identified as exemplary models

5. provide suggestions and opportunities for students to analyze, transfer, and apply the personal and/or societal values explored

6. help students to begin thinking about decisions they make and the effect these decisions have on themselves, others and society in general

OBJECTIVES

Through the use of *I Want to Be Like* students will...

1. use research skills

2. experience expository writing

3. evaluate cause/effect relationships

4. use a variety of research media (i.e., newspapers, videocassettes, and magazines)

5. generate responses in a variety of ways (i.e., written, visual and auditory)

AUDIENCE

I Want to Be Like can be successfully used by...

1. anyone interested in ethics
2. anyone learning, teaching, or using problem-solving skills
3. anyone learning, teaching, or using critical-thinking skills
4. anyone learning, teaching, or using research skills
5. anyone interested in integrating creative problem solving, thinking, and research
6. anyone interested in playing around with ideas

"Anyone" could be defined by the user of *I Want to Be Like* as...

1. average students
2. honor students
3. gifted and talented students
4. learning-disabled students
5. unmotivated students
6. students...

USE

I Want to Be Like can be used...

1. to enrich curriculum in ethical thinking
2. to introduce positive role models
3. to support/reinforce ethical decision making
4. to enrich the school curriculum
5. to extend the school curriculum
6. to replace school curriculum components
7. as directed instruction
8. as independent study
9. by students singly, in pairs, or in groups (cooperative learning)
10. as a Type III Enrichment (Renzulli)
11. as a foundation for extra-curricular enrichment programs
12. in conjunction with school counselors

Creative Problem Solving

Creative Problem Solving is a structured process for investigating the possibilities generated by a problem. The problem solver may find that he/she will develop one or several solutions. Any of the possible solutions may or may not be effective/efficient in addressing the problem. Therefore, a problem solver is, in fact, a problem seeker.

Creative Problem Solving invovles seven hierarchal steps:

Recognize The Problem	Realize that the stated problems are focused on the individual described and the value cited. (*Value* and *quality* are interchangeable.)
Define The Problem	Define the problem as a result of the interactive role of the value and the individual.
Gather Ideas/Data	Gather information/data/ideas about the value, the individual and events.
Rank Ideas/Data	Rank the ideas as a means to use the factual data about the person and make potential solutions to the problem.
Test Ideas/Data	Test solution ideas.
Draw Conclusions	Draw conclusions about products as a solution to the posed problem.
Evaluate Conclusions	Evaluate the solution as effective/efficient without violating the data base reality.

Bloom's Taxonomy

Bloom's Taxonomy* is an attempt to define the process of thinking by means of a structured hierarchy. The thinking process is believed to begin with KNOWLEDGE—i.e., awarenesss—and to progress eventually to evaluating and judging things, concepts, and ideas.

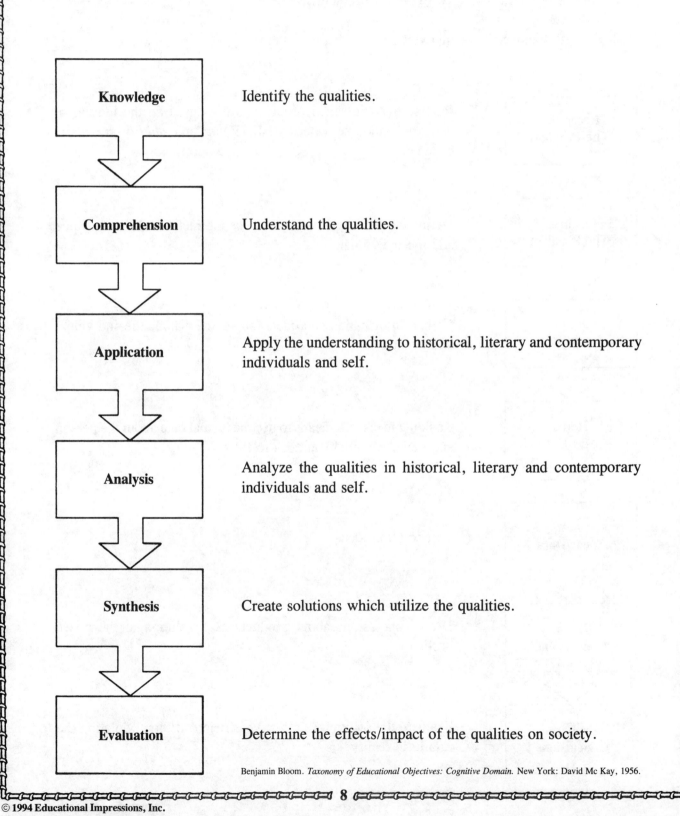

Knowledge	Identify the qualities.
Comprehension	Understand the qualities.
Application	Apply the understanding to historical, literary and contemporary individuals and self.
Analysis	Analyze the qualities in historical, literary and contemporary individuals and self.
Synthesis	Create solutions which utilize the qualities.
Evaluation	Determine the effects/impact of the qualities on society.

Benjamin Bloom. *Taxonomy of Educational Objectives: Cognitive Domain.* New York: David Mc Kay, 1956.

Research Scheme

Research is an orgainized method for investigating the unknown. The result of research may lead to a rational, logical, plausible yet possible conclusion. The conclusion, however, must be based upon a research supported data base. One possible research scheme is the following:

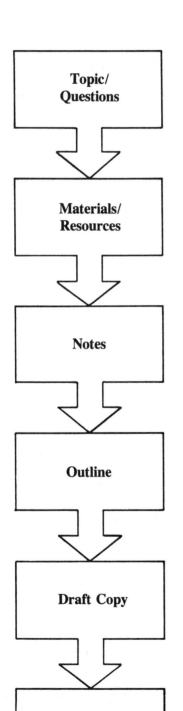

The TOPIC is the subject to be researched. It may be assigned or chosen. QUESTIONS are queries—assigned or self-selected—related to the TOPIC. (What is the thesis statement?)

The MATERIALS/RESOURCES are the sources of information to be used in researching the topic/questions. (What data do I need and where can I find it?)

NOTES are important pieces of information concerning the topic/questions taken from the materials/resources and recorded for later use. (What information do I need to record?)

The OUTLINE is a way to structure and organize the information accumulated in the NOTES. (How do I order the recorded information?)

The DRAFT is a preliminary narrative compilation of information related to the topic/questions developed from the outline. (How might I present the preliminary response to the thesis statement?)

The FINAL COPY is the product which is a response to the topic/questions posed. (Does the outcome effectively/efficiently address the thesis statement?)

Integration

Through the use of *I Want to Be Like,* students and teachers will concurrently utilize Bloom's Taxonomy, creative problem solving and some structured research scheme. Direct instruction, practice and/or a simulation experience will enable the students to feel comfortable with the three essential components.

This book provides opportunities for students to . . .
- explore exemplary models of selected values/qualities
- apply the new understanding of the values/qualities to contemporary individuals/events
- and recognize personal experiences in which the student has had a need for one or more of the value/qualities cited.

The use of CPS/Bloom/Research Scheme provides the student with the organization, process and structure to facilitate his/her understanding of the values at issue.

Integration: A Step-By-Step Guide

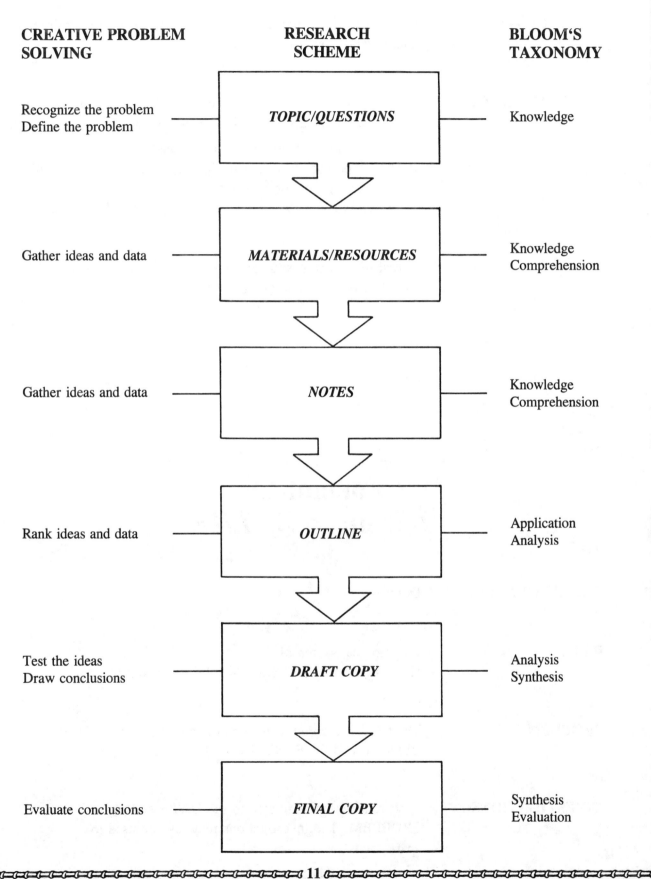

CREATIVE PROBLEM SOLVING	RESEARCH SCHEME	BLOOM'S TAXONOMY
Recognize the problem Define the problem	TOPIC/QUESTIONS	Knowledge
Gather ideas and data	MATERIALS/RESOURCES	Knowledge Comprehension
Gather ideas and data	NOTES	Knowledge Comprehension
Rank ideas and data	OUTLINE	Application Analysis
Test the ideas Draw conclusions	DRAFT COPY	Analysis Synthesis
Evaluate conclusions	FINAL COPY	Synthesis Evaluation

Definition of Terms

HISTORICAL: Individual whose biographical sketch and analysis exemplify the quality/value being examined.

CONTEMPORARY: Any current individual whose actions exemplify the quality/value being examined. The individual may be...

- a famous person, real or fictional
- a person who appears in the media (i.e., TV, radio, newspaper, or mazazine)
- a personal acquaintance, friend, or family member.

SELF: A real or potential situation wherein the student has or might have to use the quality/value examined.

Format Of
I Want to Be Like

QUALITY/VALUE: Defined.

DATA: Biographical sketch of the HISTORICAL/CONTEMPORARY/SELF figure.

PROBLEM: The task. The completion requires the integration of CPS, BLOOM, and the RESEARCH SCHEME.

INVESTIGATIONS::   Researchable topics related to the DATA and/or the PROBLEM. The investigations may also be used to spark/focus specific research.

Four Routes/Options for Exploring *I Want to Be Like*

Teachers/Students may choose any of the four routes/options listed; however, before attempting Route 4: Wild Card, the user must explore a route that begins with a HISTORICAL figure (Route 1, 2, or 3).

ROUTE 1:
1. Select a quality/value.
2. Do the Background/Research page for a HISTORICAL figure: Data, Problem, and Investigations.
3. Generate responses to the PROBLEM.

ROUTE 2:
1. Select a quality.
2. Do the Background/Research page for a HISTORICAL figure: Data, Problem and Investigations.
3. Generate responses to the PROBLEM and hold them for later use.
4. Identify a CONTEMPORARY figure and create a Background/Research page.
5. Develop a response to the CONTEMPORARY figure's PROBLEM.
6. Develop a statement which compares/contrasts the CONTEMPORARY figure with the HISTORICAL figure.

ROUTE 3:
1. Do ROUTE 2.
2. Student identifies a situation for SELF wherein the quality has or might be used.
3. Create a Background/Research page for SELF.
4. Develop responses to SELF's PROBLEM and hold them for later use.
5. Compare/contrast the similarities/differences among the responses for SELF/CONTEMPORARY/HISTORICAL figures.
6. Create a statement which identifies the significant similarities among the three figures.

ROUTE 4: WILD CARD
1. Complete at least one trip through Route 1, 2, or 3.
2. Select a QUALITY/VALUE for investigation.
3. Identify a real/fictional/contemporary/historical figure who exemplifies the QUALITY/VALUE.
4. Do a Background/Research page.
5. Generate responses to the PROBLEM.
6. BONUS: Compare/Contrast WILD CARD to any other component. (Students may use the TRANSFER/APPLICATION Analysis Component.)

FLOW CHART FOR *I WANT TO BE LIKE*

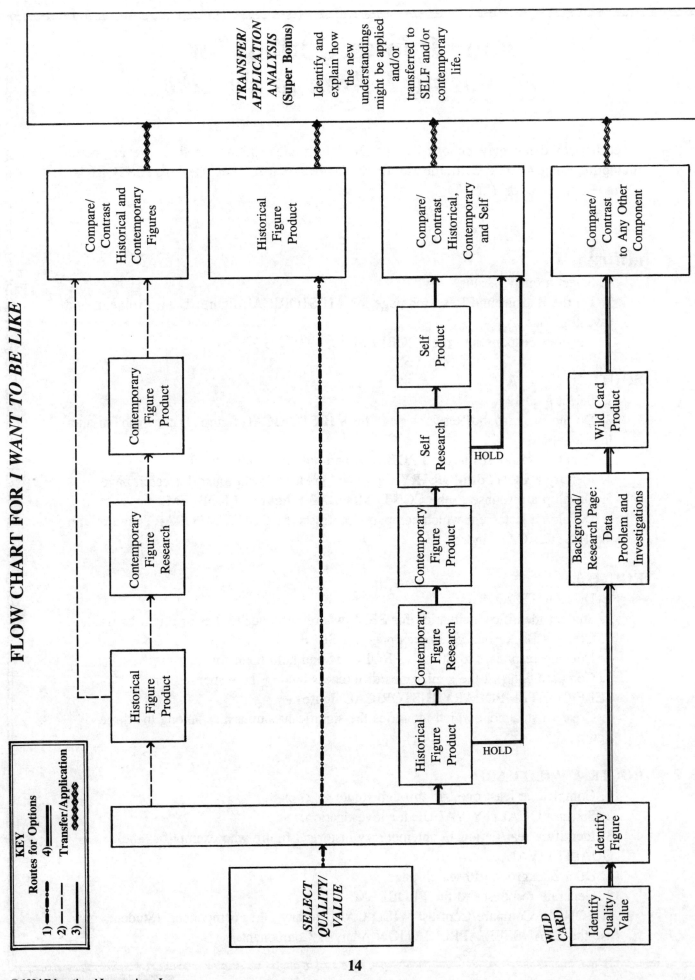

KEY

Routes for Options
1)
2)
3)
4)

Transfer/Application

TRANSFER/ APPLICATION ANALYSIS (Super Bonus) Identify and explain how the new understandings might be applied and/or transferred to SELF and/or contemporary life.

Compare/ Contrast Historical and Contemporary Figures

Contemporary Figure Product

Contemporary Figure Research

Historical Figure Product

SELECT QUALITY/ VALUE

Historical Figure Product

Compare/ Contrast Historical, Contemporary and Self

Self Product

Self Research

Contemporary Figure Product

Contemporary Figure Research

Historical Figure Product

HOLD

HOLD

Compare/ Contrast to Any Other Component

Wild Card Product

Background/ Research Page: Data Problem and Investigations

Identify Figure

Identify Quality/ Value

WILD CARD

BACKGROUND/RESEARCH

COURAGE: the quality of mind that enables one to encounter difficulties and danger with firmness or without fear; bravery.

Jack (Jackie) Roosevelt Robinson

DATA:

Jackie Robinson (1919-1972), a professional baseball player and business executive, was born in Cairo, Georgia. At the University of California he was an outstanding athlete and participated in football, basketball, baseball and track. After service in the military during World War II, he became a professional baseball player with the Kansas City Monarchs of the Negro National League. In 1945 he became part of the Brooklyn Dodgers organization, and in 1947 he was brought up from the minors to play major league ball. He thus became the first African-American in history to play major league baseball. He had a long and outstanding career in baseball with a lifetime batting average of .311. He played for six pennant winners and one championship team in Brooklyn and was elected to the Baseball Hall of Fame in 1962. After retiring from baseball, he became vice-president of the Chock Full O'Nuts coffee company and served as co-chairman of the Freedom National Bank of Harlem. He also served as an aide to Governor Nelson Rockefeller of New York and became an avid spokesperson and fundraiser for the civil rights movement.

PROBLEM:

As Jackie Robinson, write highlights from your personal diary expressing your feelings as the first African-American player in major league baseball.

INVESTIGATIONS:

1. Why did Robinson choose to attend the University of California?

2. What obstacles did Jackie Robinson face in his first year in the majors?

3. Why was it possible for Robinson to break the "color barrier" in 1947?

4. What were the ramifications to Robinson and his family on becoming the first African-American major league sports figure?

5. Why was Robinson a trusted spokesperson for the civil rights movement?

6. What impact has Jackie Robinson's courage had on opportunities for black professionals?

Simulation

Recognize the problem Define the problem	*TOPIC/ QUESTIONS*	Knowledge

WRITE HIGHLIGHTS FROM YOUR PERSONAL DIARY
EXPRESSING YOUR FEELINGS AS THE FIRST
AFRICAN-AMERICAN IN MAJOR LEAGUE BASEBALL.

          Topic: Courage/Jack (Jackie) Roosevelt Robinson
Investigations::   Who?
                    What?
                    Where?
                    When?
                    Why?
                    So what?

Gather ideas and data	*MATERIALS/ RESOURCES*	Knowledge Comprehension

Appropriate to the TOPIC: Courage/Jackie Robinson

Robinson, civil rights, courage, baseball
Kansas City Monarchs, Dodgers,
Baseball Hall of Fame, Chock Full O'Nuts

Sources: Encyclopedias, magazines, biographies, film archives,
          videocassettes, filmstrips, dictionaries, texts, trade books,
          television, pamphlets

Gather ideas and data	*NOTES*	Knowledge Comprehension

To be taken in a format appropriate to the TOPIC: key words, phrases, sentences to support possible diary entries

Note cards

Rank ideas and data	*OUTLINE*	Application Analysis

I. Life after baseball
   A.
   B.
   C.

II. Professional years in baseball
   A.
   B.
   C.

III. Entry year into professional baseball
   A.
   B.
   C.

IV. Minor League ball
   A.
   B.
   C.

V. Personal history before baseball
   A.
   B.
   C.

Test the ideas Draw conclusions	*DRAFT* *COPY*	Analysis Synthesis

Develop preliminary diary

Diary may be designed in reverse chronological order, chronological order, stream of consciousness, collection of personal notes, scrapbook, etc.

Evaluate conclusions	*FINAL* *COPY*	Synthesis Evaluation

Determine the best format for the diary.
Create the diary.
Does the diary effectively and efficiently solve the problem?

Transfer/Application Analysis

The purpose of pursuing a transfer/application analysis is to enable students to realize that the decisions they make can be supported by knowing historical and contemporary figures who may have faced similar dilemmas.

From this section, have students choose one of the HISTORICAL figures they have researched. Have them identify one CONTEMPORARY figure who exemplifies the same quality as the HISTORICAL figure. Students should then decide on a personal situation where they might apply the same quality as these HISTORICAL/CONTEMPORARY figures.

For the IF cells:
1. List EVENTS which enable each individual to exhibit the quality.
2. List key ACTIONS of each individual which exemplify the use of the quality.
3. List plausible REASONS for key ACTIONS made by each individual.
4. Identify the EFFECTS of the key ACTION made by each individual.

For the THEN cells:
1. Determine and record SIMILARITIES common to all three individuals.
2. Identify and record DIFFERENCES.

For the THEREFORE cells:
1. Draw conclusions about...

   - the quality/value
   - the individuals
   - the events
   - the key actions
   - the reasons
   - the effect/affect
   on YOU as an individual.
2. Record responses.

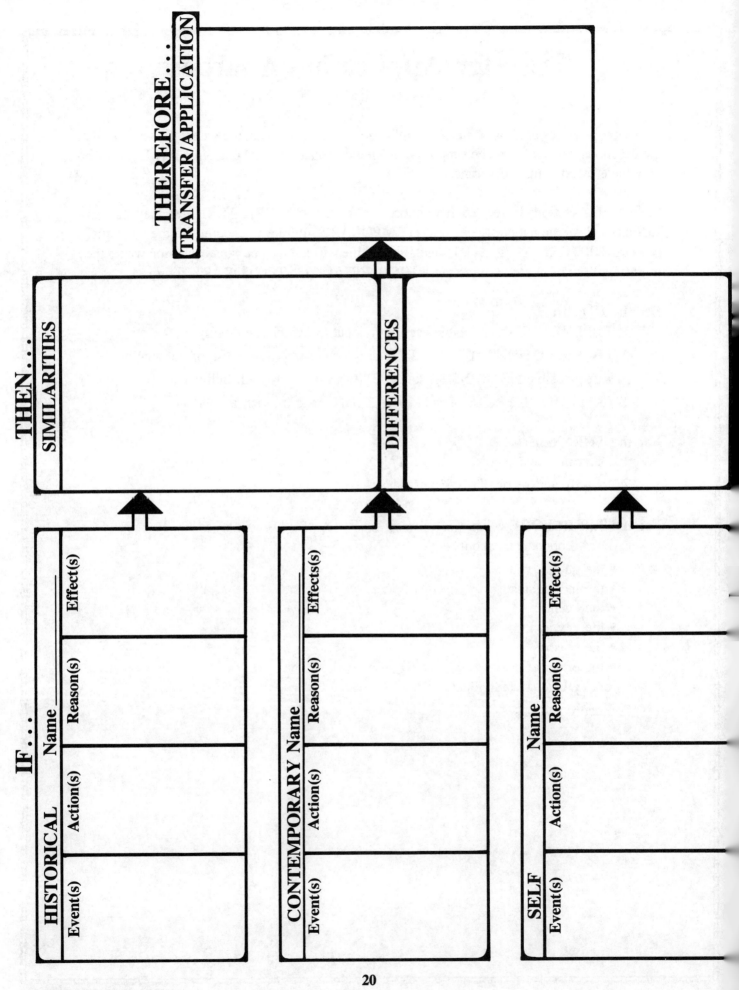

THEREFORE...
TRANSFER/APPLICATION

THEN...
SIMILARITIES

DIFFERENCES

IF...

HISTORICAL Name

Event(s)	Action(s)	Reason(s)	Effect(s)

CONTEMPORARY Name

Event(s)	Action(s)	Reason(s)	Effects(s)

SELF Name

Event(s)	Action(s)	Reason(s)	Effect(s)

THEN...

SIMILARITIES

- Showed courage
- got rewards
- action affected broader audience

DIFFERENCES

- not all for personal gain
- different circumstances
- spontaneous vs. planned
- personal vs. external reasons

- the result of a courageous act can have an effect on many people
- successfully facing adversity can change the life of the courageous person
- result is worth the risk

HISTORICAL Name *Jackie Robinson*

Event(s)	Action(s)	Reason(s)	Effect(s)
• played college sports	• played pro-ball with whites	• Civil rights	• broke color line for all
• played for Kansas City Monarchs	• broke the color line in pro-ball	• Career move	• made political/social/economic progress for self and others
• broke records		• personal income	

CONTEMPORARY Name *Sam Edwards*

Event(s)	Action(s)	Reason(s)	Effects(s)
• working across from bridge	• finds ladder	• just seemed right	• people rescued
• earthquake	• climbs into rubble	• people hurt	• Sam gets recognition from press/community
• bridge collapses—people trapped	• searches for and rescues people	• others more important than self	

SELF Name *Raymond Curtis*

Event(s)	Action(s)	Reason(s)	Effect(s)
• beaten up on bus	• rode bus anyway	• had to get to school	• big guys backed down
• threatened by big kids	• took up weight-lifting	• wanted to ride, not walk	• girl noticed Raymond
• book/money stolen	• stared bullies down	• liked a girl on the bus	• other kids hung around Ray for safety

21

Gather
LOYALTY
GENEROSITY
PERSEVERANCE
realize
Rank
Draw conclusions
SELF
Action(s)
Analysis
Develop
Test the ideas
DRAFT
Investigations
situation
A Step-By-Step Guide
exhibit
CONTEMPORARY
HONESTY
consciousness
Synthesis
Value
HISTORICAL
Event(s)
WRITE
Data
DIFFERENCES
Reason
personal notes
individual
Simulation
HIGHLIGHTS
exemplify
SELECT
QUALITY/VALUE
TRANSFER/APPLICATION
decide
Objectives
WILD
Test
SCHEME
QUESTIONS
CARD
Conclusions
Integration
THEREFORE
Define
Creative
Routes
TOPIC
COURAGE
Identify
Exploration
Knowledge
Ideas
Honesty
PROBLEM
SIMILARITIES
RESEARCH
Analysis
Goals
RESPECT
Recognize
information
COMMITMENT
Effect(s)

BACKGROUND/RESEARCH

LOYALTY: the quality of being faithful to an ideal, cause, custom or person; fidelity; allegiance; devotion.

Annie Sullivan

DATA:

Annie Sullivan (1866-1936) was hired from the Perkins Institution in Boston on March 2, 1887, by the parents of Helen Keller to be Helen's teacher. Helen was a young child who was both deaf and blind. Annie Sullivan remained with Helen as mentor and friend until her own death in 1936. As her teacher, Ms. Sullivan made contact with Helen Keller's mind through the sense of touch. She spelled words in Helen's palm and taught her to speak by allowing Helen to put fingers on her larynx in order to ''hear'' the vibrations. In 1890 Annie went with Helen to the Horace Mann School for the Deaf, where Helen learned to read and write Braille. In 1900 Ms. Sullivan accompanied Helen Keller to Radcliffe College. She interpreted the lectures and class discussions by spelling the words into her hands. Ms. Sullivan remained there with Helen until 1904 when Helen graduated with honors. In 1905 Annie married John A. Macy, a literary critic, but she remained Helen's loyal companion until her death.

PROBLEM:

Hypothesize what Helen Keller's life might have been like without the loyalty of Annie Sullivan.

INVESTIGATIONS:

1. Why did the Kellers hire someone from the Perkins Institution?

2. Why did Annie continue to work with Helen after the breakthrough?

3. What was the breakthrough?

4. What skills did Annie bring to her involvement with Helen?

5. What sacrifices might Annie Sullivan have made in order to remain loyal to Helen Keller?

BACKGROUND/RESEARCH

LOYALTY: the quality of being faithful to an ideal, cause, custom or person; fidelity; allegiance; devotion.

Matthew A. Henson

DATA:

Matthew A. Henson (1866-1955), son of an African-American tenant farmer, was a polar explorer. In 1887 Robert E. Peary hired Henson as his personal servant to accompany him on a surveying expedition to Nicaragua. Proving himself resourceful and indispensable, in 1891 Henson was engaged by Peary not as a servant, but as a member of the expedition to the North Pole. Henson accompanied Peary to the polar region in 1900, 1902, 1905 and 1908. Henson related well to the Eskimos, skillfully handled the equipment and dogs, and gave moral support to his companion, Robert Peary. Fighting snowblindedness, frostbite, and physical exhaustion, Henson and Peary reached the North Pole on April 6, 1909. Matthew Henson placed the American flag on the point of the North Pole.

PROBLEM:

Determine how Matthew Henson dealt with Peary's acclaim following their shared experiences. Explain.

INVESTIGATIONS:

1. Why did Henson agree to work for Peary?

2. When and how did Henson's role change from servant to compansion?

3. What qualities did Henson have that enabled him to be a successful explorer?

4. What were the implications of Henson placing the United States flag on the North Pole?

5. What was the importance of Henson's ability to communicate with the Eskimos?

6. Why did Henson stay with Peary through all the hardships?

7. What value did Henson's loyalty have to Peary's success?

BACKGROUND/RESEARCH

LOYALTY: the quality of being faithful to an ideal, cause, custom or person; fidelity; allegiance; devotion.

Nathan Hale

DATA:

Nathan Hale (1755-1776) was a patriot and hero of the American Revolution. A graduate of Yale, Hale taught school until he received a lieutenant's commission and helped in the siege of Boston. Hale was always outspoken about his belief in freedom for the colonies and gave speeches in favor of liberty. In 1776, when George Washington needed information about the enemy, Hale volunteered for hazardous spy duty behind the British lines on Long Island. He was to pose as a schoolmaster and obtain maps and other information. On September 21 he was captured by the British. Secret documents were found on Hale and he had no choice but to confess. Prior to his hanging the following morning, Hale said, "I only regret that I have but one life to lose for my country."

PROBLEM:

Compare Nathan Hale's concept of loyalty to that of a fictional or non-fictional spy character.

INVESTIGATIONS:

1. What qualities might George Washington have looked for in Nathan Hale?

2. Why did Hale pose as a schoolmaster?

3. What are covert operations? Why are they sometimes necessary in wartime?

4. Was Hale's loyalty worth the price? Why?

5. What effect did Hale's loyalty have on the outcome of the American Revolution? What are the implications of your feelings?

6. Does deception in the name of loyalty ever become destructive? When?

LOYALTY: the quality of being faithful to an ideal, cause, custom or person; fidelity; allegiance; devotion.

Louis Howe

DATA:

Louis Howe (1871-1936), a newspaper man in Albany, New York, was committed to the political advancement and future of his friend Franklin Delano Roosevelt. From behind the scenes, Howe ran FDR's 1912 campaign for re-election to the New York State Senate. He also influenced FDR's political development as governor of New York in 1928 and 1930 and as President of the United States in 1932. When FDR was stricken with polio in 1921, Louis Howe worked with Eleanor Roosevelt around the clock to care for him. Howe's devotion included moving his wife and two children to Washington to become the President's personal secretary. Howe taught Eleanor a lot about politics so that she could not only support her husband in office, but also become an influential woman of the world in her own right. As President, FDR said of Louis, "There are two people in the United States more than anybody who are responsible for this victory. One is my old friend and associate Colonel Louis McHenry Howe."

PROBLEM:

As FDR, write a speech honoring Louis Howe's loyalty in helping you attain the office of President of the United States.

INVESTIGATIONS:

1. How and why did Howe become so politically influential?

2. Why did Howe stay loyal to FDR even after FDR became handicapped?

3. In what way did Howe's loyalty support Eleanor's developing career?

4. When and in what way did Howe first become part of the FDR entourage?

5. In what way did Howe's loyalty to FDR effect his own newspaper career?

6. What might have happened if Howe had not remained loyal to FDR prior to his election to the Presidency?

LOYALTY: the quality of being faithful to an ideal, cause, custom or person; fidelity; allegiance; devotion.

Sacajawea (Bird Woman)

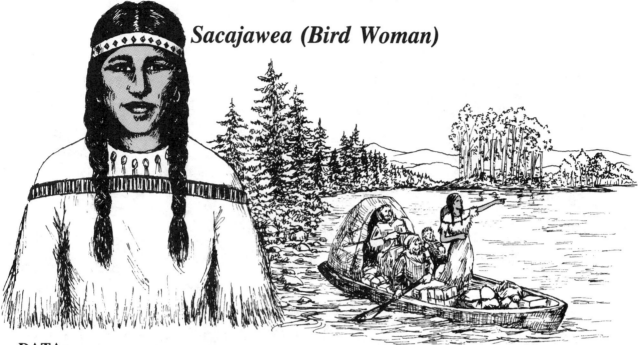

DATA:

Sacajawea (1787?-1812?) was a Native American woman, best known for her help to Meriwether Lewis and William Clark on their famed expedition. A member of the Snake tribe of the Shoshone Indians, she was captured by an enemy tribe and sold to a Canadian trapper, whom she later married. She and her husband were hired by the explorers Lewis and Clark. They acted as guides and interpreters on Lewis and Clark's expedition to the Pacific Coast. While on their difficult trek, Sacajawea was able to make contact with the Shoshone tribe and helped Lewis and Clark obtain much needed horses for the continuation of their journey. Knowing that the hardest part of the journey lay ahead through the Rocky Mountains, Sacajawea again left her native people to remain loyal to Lewis and Clark in their search for the Pacific Ocean. Sacajawea has been honored by having a mountain pass, a peak, and rivers named after her.

PROBLEM:

Compare how the white settlers and the Native American people would evaluate the impact of Sacajawea's loyalty.

INVESTIGATIONS:

1. Why might Sacajawea have decided to stay with Lewis and Clark after she had been re-united with the Shoshone?

2. What difficulties were Lewis and Clark able to avoid because of Sacajawea's loyalty?

3. What happened to Sacajawea after the Lewis and Clark Expedition? Why?

4. Why would Lewis and Clark have chosen a woman as a guide for their expedition?

5. What impact did her loyalty to the white men have on the Native American population?

BACKGROUND/RESEARCH

LOYALTY: the quality of being faithful to an ideal, cause, custom or person; fidelity; allegiance; devotion.

*Wilbur**

DATA:

Wilbur (Spring...) is a pig, the runt of the litter, born on the Arable farm. He narrowly escapes the usual fate of runts by becoming the pet of the youngest child of the farm's owner. When he becomes too large to be a household pet, he is sent to the Zuckerman farm and finds it difficult to make friends in the new barnyard. Charlotte, a spider, befriends him and because of her loyalty to him, she is able to engineer a way for Wilbur to survive. Despite difficulties and obstacles, Wilbur, in turn, proves to be a true and loyal friend to Charlotte as well.

from *Charlotte's Web*, by E.B. White

PROBLEM:

As one of the barnyard animals at the Zuckerman farm, write an article for the *Farmer's Almanac* predicting the impact of Wilbur's and Charlotte's loyalty on the other barnyard residents.

INVESTIGATIONS:

1. How and why did Charlotte become friendly?

2. How did Wilbur and Charlotte show their loyalty to each other?

3. What was Charlotte's engineering feat?

4. What sacrifice did Charlotte make because of her loyalty?

5. How did Wilbur's expression of loyalty affect his character?

6. What is the legacy of Wilbur's loyalty to Charlotte?

TRANSFER/APPLICATION

Loyalty

LOYALTY: the quality of being faithful to an ideal, cause, custom or person; fidelity; allegiance; devotion.

IDENTIFY SOMEONE WHO EXEMPLIFIES LOYALTY.
THE PERSON MAY BE FICTIONAL OR NON-FICTIONAL.

(name)

(graphic)

DATA:

PROBLEM:

INVESTIGATIONS:

1. What were the significant events of _____'s life?

2. Why were these events significant?

3. How might _____ have defined loyalty? How would you define loyalty?

4. Did _____'s response to the events of his/her life match his/her definition of loyalty? Do they match yours?

5. How did _____'s response to events in his/her life demonstrate his/her loyalty?

6. What event tested _____'s loyalty the most? Why?

TRANSFER/APPLICATION

Loyalty

LOYALTY: the quality of being faithful to an ideal, cause, custom or person; fidelity; allegiance; devotion.

USING YOURSELF, SHOW HOW YOU HAVE EXEMPLIFIED OR EXEMPLIFY LOYALTY.

(your name)

(graphic)

DATA:

PROBLEM:

INVESTIGATIONS:

1. What significant event(s) of your life required you to be loyal?

2. Why were these events significant? Why were you loyal?

3. Does your response to the events of your life match your definition of loyalty?

4. How did your response to events in your life demonstrate your loyalty?

5. What event tested your loyalty the most?

BACKGROUND/RESEARCH

COURAGE: the quality of mind that enables one to encounter difficulties and danger with firmness or without fear; bravery.

Jack (Jackie) Roosevelt Robinson

DATA:

Jackie Robinson (1919-1972), a professional baseball player and business executive, was born in Cairo, Georgia. At the University of California he was an outstanding athlete and participated in football, basketball, baseball and track. After service in the military during World War II, he became a professional baseball player with the Kansas City Monarchs of the Negro National League. In 1945 he became part of the Brooklyn Dodgers organization, and in 1947 he was brought up from the minors to play major league ball. He thus became the first African-American in history to play major league baseball. He had a long and outstanding career in baseball with a lifetime batting average of .311. He played for six pennant winners and one championship team in Brooklyn and was elected to the Baseball Hall of Fame in 1962. After retiring from baseball, he became vice-president of the Chock Full O'Nuts coffee company and served as co-chairman of the Freedom National Bank of Harlem. He also served as an aide to Governor Nelson Rockefeller of New York and became an avid spokesperson and fundraiser for the civil rights movement.

PROBLEM:

As Jackie Robinson, write highlights from your personal diary expressing your feelings as the first African-American player in major league baseball.

INVESTIGATIONS:

1. Why did Robinson choose to attend the University of California?

2. What obstacles did Jackie Robinson face in his first year in the majors?

3. Why was it possible for Robinson to break the "color barrier" in 1947?

4. What were the ramifications to Robinson and his family on becoming the first African-American major league sports figure?

5. Why was Robinson a trusted spokesperson for the civil rights movement?

6. What impact has Jackie Robinson's courage had on opportunities for black professionals?

BACKGROUND/RESEARCH

COURAGE: the quality of mind that enables one to encounter difficulties and danger with firmness or without fear; bravery.

Charles A. Lindbergh

DATA:

Charles Lindbergh (1902-1974) was an American aviator. He made the first solo flight across the Atlantic Ocean in a single-engine plane. Lindbergh took off in the *Spirit of St. Louis* from Roosevelt Field in New York at 7:52 A.M. on May 20, 1927, and landed at Le Bourget Field near Paris, France, the next day. He flew more than 3,000 miles in 33⅓ hours. His courageous flight opened the era of trans-Atlantic air travel.

PROBLEM:

Describe how Lindbergh's courage helped him through the remainder of his life.

INVESTIGATIONS:

1. What were the significant events of Lindbergh's life?

2. Why were these events significant?

3. How might Lindbergh have defined courage? How would you define courage?

4. Did Lindbergh's response to the events of his life match his definition of courage? Do they match yours?

5. How did Lindbergh's response to events in his life demonstrate his courage?

6. What event tested Lindbergh's courage the most? Why?

BACKGROUND/RESEARCH

COURAGE: the quality of mind that enables one to encounter difficulties and danger with firmness or without fear; bravery.

Mary Ludwig Hays McCauley (Molly Pitcher)

DATA:

Mary Ludwig Hays McCauley (1754-1832), better known as Molly Pitcher, served heroically in the American Revolution. Mary was servant to a doctor prior to her marriage to John Hays. Hays, a barber, enlisted in the First Pennsylvania Artillery as a gunner. Mary traveled with him and she received ½ rations for washing, cooking and sewing for the Continental Army. She carried water to the tired and wounded soldiers, thereby earning her nickname, Molly Pitcher. In 1778, when Mary's husband suffered from heat exhaustion, Mary manned his cannon through the Battle of Monmouth. For her courageous services, the Pennsylvania Assembly awarded her a pension of $40.00 a year for life.

PROBLEM:

Explain the courageous role Molly Pitcher played in the American Revolution and compare it with women's roles in other wars in which the United States took part.

INVESTIGATIONS:

1. Why would Molly Pitcher take part in the American Revolution with her husband?

2. How and why did Molly Pitcher end up in combat?

3. What was the effect of Molly Pitcher's courageous acts on the Battle of Monmouth? On the war?

4. What hardships would Molly Pitcher have had to deal with during the American Revolution?

5. Were other women involved in the American Revolution? Why was Molly's courage singled out?

6. After showing such courage in battle, why would Molly Pitcher not be given a military leadership role?

TRANSFER/APPLICATION

Courage

COURAGE: the quality of mind that enables one to encounter difficulties and danger with firmness or without fear; bravery.

IDENTIFY SOMEONE WHO EXEMPLIFIES COURAGE. THE PERSON MAY BE FICTIONAL OR NON-FICTIONAL.

(name)

(graphic)

DATA:

PROBLEM:

INVESTIGATIONS:

1. What were the significant events of _____'s life?

2. Why were these events significant?

3. How might _____ have defined courage? How would you define courage?

4. Did _____'s response to the events of his/her life match his/her definition of courage? Do they match yours?

5. How did _____'s response to events in his/her life demonstrate his/her courage?

6. What event tested _____'s courage the most? Why?

Courage

COURAGE: the quality of mind that enables one to encounter difficulties and danger with firmness or without fear; bravery.

USING YOURSELF, SHOW HOW YOU HAVE EXEMPLIFIED OR EXEMPLIFY COURAGE.

(your name)

(graphic)

DATA:

PROBLEM:

INVESTIGATIONS:

1. What significant event(s) of your life required you to be courageous?

2. Why were these events significant? Why were you courageous?

3. Does your response to the events of your life match your definition of courage?

4. How did your response to events in your life demonstrate your courage?

5. What event tested your courage the most?

BACKGROUND/RESEARCH

HONESTY: the quality of being truthful; refraining from lying, cheating or stealing; fair, sincere, straightforward.

Lillian Hellman

DATA:

Lillian Hellman (1905-) is an American writer of plays and screenplays. Honesty is the theme of many of Ms. Hellman's works. Her most memorable include *The Children's Hour, The Little Foxes* and *The Dark Angel.* From 1950-1954 Senator Joseph McCarthy accused many people, particularly those in the arts, of subversive (Communist) activities. People were encouraged to accuse others and to give names to a congressional committee. As a result, many writers, actors, directors and others lost their jobs and were "blacklisted"; some even went to jail. In 1952 Ms. Hellman was called before the House Committee on Un-American Activities. She upheld a private honor and would not name any others. She courageously stated, "I cannot and will not cut my conscience to fit this year's fashions."

PROBLEM:

Compare what might have been Senator McCarthy's definition of private honor with Lillian Hellman's definition.

INVESTIGATIONS:

1. What events in Lillian Hellman's background and upbringing helped develop her attitude toward fairness?

2. Explain why McCarthy targeted the arts community?

3. What was blacklisting and what were some of the ramifications of being blacklisted?

4. How was Lillian Hellman's personal life affected by the McCarthy hearings?

5. How would Lillian Hellman define private honor?

6. Investigate how Hellman's work showed honesty as a theme.

HONESTY: the quality of being truthful; refraining from lying, cheating or stealing; fair, sincere, straightforward.

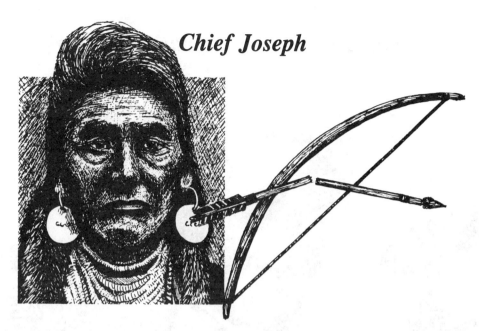

Chief Joseph

DATA:

Chief Joseph (1840?-1904) was the Nez Perce who became an important leader, not so much for his prowess in battle as for his great strength of character and intelligence. He led his people in their unsuccessful attempt to have the rights that were given to them in their 1855 treaty with the United States government enforced. The U.S. government tried to force the Nez Perce to sign a new treaty accepting a new, much smaller reservation. Chief Joseph asked that Native Americans be allowed the basic freedoms they had enjoyed long before the white settlers had arrived. Although he finally agreed to give up their land, believing it was better to "live at peace than to begin a war and lie dead," a series of raids on both sides led to war. Chief Joseph proved to be an able military leader, but in the end the Nez Perces were forced to leave their homes and relocate in Indian Territory (Oklahoma). In 1885 Chief Joseph and several of his followers were taken to the Colville Indian Reservation in Washington State. Chief Joseph died there in 1904.

PROBLEM:

Analyze why people said that Chief Joseph died of a broken heart.

INVESTIGATIONS:

1. What were the significant events surrounding Chief Joseph's leadership of the Nez Perces?

2. Why did the United States government want the land?

3. Why would negotiations between the United States government and the Nez Perces over land ownership be difficult?

4. Were Chief Joseph's requests fair? Why? Why not? For whom?

5. How might Chief Joseph have defined honesty? Why? How would you define honesty?

6. How does Chief Joseph's speech which includes the line "I will fight no more forever" reveal his honesty?

BACKGROUND/RESEARCH

HONESTY: the quality of being truthful; refraining from lying, cheating or stealing; fair, sincere, straightforward.

Isabella Baumfree (Sojourner Truth)

DATA:

Born in New York, Isabella Baumfree (1793-1883), better known as Sojourner Truth, was known as the Pilgrim of Freedom. She was the first African-American woman to speak out publicly against slavery. She also spoke in favor of woman's suffrage. Born a slave, she was freed in 1828. In 1843 she received what she described as a command from God to travel and preach about the need to abolish slavery. She left New York and took the name Sojourner Truth. Although beaten and stoned, Sojourner Truth, through her strong character, intelligence, wit and the sincerity of her speeches, continued to proclaim the truth about the injustice of slavery throughout the United States. In 1864 she met with President Lincoln and worked to improve living conditions in Washington, D.C. Isabella Baumfree lived up to her chosen name.

PROBLEM:

Create a dialogue between President Lincoln and Sojourner Truth at their meeting in 1864. The dialogue should reflect the truth as she saw it.

INVESTIGATIONS:

1. How did Sojourner Truth define truth? Be specific.

2. With which of Sojourner Truth's points would President Lincoln have agreed?

3. With which would he have not agreed? Why?

4. Why was abolition such a controversial issue at that time?

5. List other people who spoke out and supported abolition.

BACKGROUND/RESEARCH

HONESTY: the quality of being truthful; refraining from lying, cheating or stealing; fair, sincere, straightforward.

Anne Shirley*

DATA:

Anne Shirley is a charming, spirited, creative, red-haired girl. She is an orphan who has been placed on a farm on Prince Edward Island. The farm is owned by a spinster and her elderly bachelor brother who had requested a boy to help with the farm chores. Despite some initial trials and tribulations, Anne stays with the Cuthberts. Always honest, Anne says what she thinks, which frequently gets her into trouble with a variety of people. Eventually, however, Anne enriches all of their lives.

*from *Anne of Green Gables,* by Lucy Maud Montgomery

PROBLEM:

Develop and present a monologue in which Anne discusses the importance of honesty to friendship.

INVESTIGATIONS:

1. How and why did honesty often get Anne into trouble?

2. Why was honesty so important to Anne?

3. How did honesty affect Anne's relationship with the Cuthberts? With Gilbert? With Diana?

4. What lessons did Anne learn?

5. Compare Anne Shirley to a female character in a contemporary novel.

TRANSFER/APPLICATION

Honesty

HONESTY: the quality of being truthful; refraining from lying, cheating or stealing; fair, sincere, straightforward.

IDENTIFY SOMEONE WHO EXEMPLIFIES HONESTY.
THE PERSON MAY BE FICTIONAL OR NON-FICTIONAL.

(name)

(graphic)

DATA:

PROBLEM:

INVESTIGATIONS:

1. What were the significant events of _____'s life?

2. Why were these events significant?

3. How might _____ have defined honesty? How would you define honesty?

4. Did _____'s response to the events of his/her life match his/her definition of honesty? Do they match yours?

5. How did _____'s response to events in his/her life demonstrate his/her honesty?

6. What event tested _____'s honesty the most? Why?

TRANSFER/APPLICATION

Honesty

HONESTY: the quality of mind that enables one to encounter difficulties and danger with firmness or without fear; bravery.

USING YOURSELF, SHOW HOW YOU HAVE EXEMPLIFIED OR EXEMPLIFY HONESTY.

(your name)

(graphic)

DATA:

PROBLEM:

INVESTIGATIONS:

1. What significant event(s) of your life required you to be honest?

2. Why were these events significant? Why were you honest?

3. Does your response to the events of your life match your definition of honesty?

4. How did your response to events in your life demonstrate your honesty?

5. What event tested your honesty the most?

BACKGROUND/RESEARCH

PERSEVERANCE: the quality of steadily following a course of action; tenacity.

Thomas Alva Edison

DATA:

Thomas Alva Edison (1847-1931) was an American inventor who held the patent to more than 1,100 inventions. He thrived on work and throughout his life he was known to spend most of his time in his laboratory. His description of genius was "1 percent inspiration and 99 percent perspiration." Failure to develop positive results with a storage battery provoked this statement: "Why, I have not failed. I've just found 10,000 ways that will not work." His inventions ranged from improving devices already in use, such as the stock ticker, to completely new and original ideas, such as the phonograph. Edison was determined to create things that were needed and useful. He spent two years searching the world from the Amazon to Japan for a material that would successfully give light when charged with electricity. His success while fooling around with everything from the red hair of a beard to lampblack and tar finally led him to be known as the Wizard of Menlo Park. Never satisfied until his inventions became practical, Edison continued to work on the distribution of power for the electric light by creating the first electric power station.

PROBLEM:

Determine and explain the events in Edison's life which influenced him to become such a tenacious person.

INVESTIGATIONS:

1. Explain Edison's definition of genius.

2. How might Edison have defined perseverance?

3. How long did Edison spend working on the light bulb? Why?

4. Explain how rewards affected Edison's continued inventive perseverance.

5. How does Edison exemplify the idea that inventions create necessities?

6. Whom would Edison include in a Tenacity Club? Why?

BACKGROUND/RESEARCH

PERSEVERANCE: the quality of steadily following a course of action; tenacity.

Sir Richard Burton

DATA:

Sir Richard Burton (1821-1890) was a British explorer, adventurer, author and expert in languages. He was a British officer in the Indian Army from 1842 to 1861. In 1853, dressed in disguise as a Muslim, Burton visited the holy Muslim shrine in Mecca, a feat unsuccessfully tried by other Europeans. Because of his great interest in Arab culture and his excellent linguistic ability, Burton translated Arabic literature into English, including the great work *The Arabian Nights.* He traveled and explored on five continents and is remembered for his search with fellow explorer John Hanning Speke for the source of the Nile River. Speke and Burton became the first Europeans to see Lake Tanganyika in central Africa. The journey was treacherous and dangerous and required great physical stamina and courage. In 1860 Burton wrote the classic book on African exploration, called *Lake Regions of Central Africa.* At the end of his life he served as a British diplomat to Brazil, Syria, and Italy.

PROBLEM:

Write a resume for Sir Richard Burton to be sent with his application to be considered for the job of director of the Mars exploration team.

INVESTIGATIONS:

1. What dangers and obstacles did Burton face during his explorations?

2. What prompted Burton to begin and to continue his exploration in Africa?

3. What is the connection between the quality of perseverance and translating the true meaning of literature into other languages?

4. What personal/professional/global rewards resulted for Burton as a result of his perseverance? Explain.

5. What role might Burton play in today's situation in the Middle East?

6. How did Burton deal with the reality that although he had persevered in his explorations, recognition was given to John Hanning Speke for finding the source of the Nile?

BACKGROUND/RESEARCH

PERSEVERANCE: the quality of steadily following a course of action; tenacity.

Jane Goodall

DATA:

Born in London, Jane Goodall (1834-) is an ethologist, a scientist who studies animal behavior. She is best known for her work with chimpanzees in the wild. In 1960, as a result of the guidance of her mentor, Dr. Louis Leakey, she began working at the Gombe Stream Reserve in northwestern Tanzania. Braving the dangers of the jungle and persevering for over 28 years, she observed, studied, and wrote detailed reports about the behavior of chimpanzees in their natural habitat and discovered new information about them. Because chimps and humans are biologically very closely related, everything learned would help the world learn more about how our own Stone Age ancestors lived. What she learned also taught us how to improve life for animals. In 1965 Jane Goodall—without an undergraduate degree—earned her doctorate degree from Cambridge University. She founded the Gombe Stream Research Center and the Jane Goodall Institute for Wildlife Research, Education and Conservation. She has written many books, received many awards, and gained world-wide recognition as a great zoologist.

PROBLEM:

Create a timeline which proves Jane Goodall's quality of perseverance by illustrating the extended study conducted by her over her entire career.

INVESTIGATIONS:

1. What were the significant findings made by Goodall?

2. Explain the obstacles to her research.

3. What has been the impact of Goodall's work on the treatment of chimps as well as other animals?

4. How is it possible for a contemporary person without an undergraduate degree from college to be accepted as an expert in a field?

5. In what ways did Louis Leakey influence Jane Goodall?

BACKGROUND/RESEARCH

PERSEVERANCE: the quality of steadily following a course of action; tenacity.

*Karana**

DATA:

In the early 1800's Karana, a courageous, resourceful Native American girl, was marooned on the outermost of the Channel Islands near California. After having been accidentally left on the island, she had to learn to survive on her own and to endure the hardships of nature, loneliness, and terror. Over the eighteen years of her isolation, she accepted her fate, persevered, and became known as the "Lost Woman of San Nicolas."

*from Island of the Blue Dolphins, by Scott O'Dell

PROBLEM:

Compare and contrast how the perseverance of Karana and Robinson Crusoe enabled each to survive the hardships encountered.

INVESTIGATIONS:

1. How did Karana get stranded on the island?

2. How did she learn to understand, appreciate, and use the environment? What about Robinson Crusoe?

3. When and how, in Karana's experience, did perseverance help her to overcome fear and loneliness?

4. What other admirable traits did Karana exemplify and use in order to survive.

5. What were the positive personal outcomes of the experience for Karana? For Crusoe?

TRANSFER/APPLICATION

Perseverance

PERSEVERANCE: the quality of steadily following a course of action; tenacity.

IDENTIFY SOMEONE WHO EXEMPLIFIES PERSEVERANCE.
THE PERSON MAY BE FICTIONAL OR NON-FICTIONAL.

(name)

(graphic)

DATA:

PROBLEM:

INVESTIGATIONS:

1. What were the significant events of _____'s life?

2. Why were these events significant?

3. How might _____ have defined perseverance? How would you define perseverance?

4. Did _____'s response to the events of his/her life match his/her definition of perseverance? Do they match yours?

5. How did _____'s response to events in his/her life demonstrate his/her perseverance?

6. What event tested _____'s perseverance the most? Why?

TRANSFER/APPLICATION

Perseverance

PERSEVERANCE: the quality of steadily following a course of action; tenacity.

USING YOURSELF, SHOW HOW YOU HAVE EXEMPLIFIED OR EXEMPLIFY PERSEVERANCE.

(your name)

(graphic)

DATA:

PROBLEM:

INVESTIGATIONS:

1. What significant event(s) of your life required you to persevere?

2. Why were these events significant? Why did you persevere?

3. Does your response to the events of your life match your definition of perseverance?

4. How did your response to events in your life demonstrate your perseverance?

5. What event tested your perseverance the most?

COMMITMENT: the quality of making and keeping a pledge to follow a course of action or to support a policy or person.

Mary Harris "Mother" Jones

DATA:

Born in Ireland, Mary Harris "Mother" Jones (1830-1930) became a speaker, agitator, and organizer for the labor movement in the United States. She taught school in Michigan and Tennessee and in 1861 she married George Jones, a member of the Iron Molders' Union. Tragically, in 1867 she lost her husband and four children to yellow fever. She moved to Chicago and opened up a dress shop, but it was destroyed by fire. Mother Jones became a union organizer and founded the labor union called the Industrial Workers of the World. She convinced coal miners and other laborers to strike for better working conditions, higher wages, and shorter working hours. Mother Jones was jailed for leading miners' strikes in West Virginia in 1902 and 1913 and in Colorado in 1913 and 1914. At over eighty years of age she was still very active! Her commitment never wavered. "I am not afraid of the pen, or the scaffold, or the sword. I shall tell the truth wherever I please."

PROBLEM:

Compare the commitment needed to create a union in the early 20th century with doing the same thing in the later 20th century.

INVESTIGATIONS:

1. What is a union and what is its purpose?

2. Explain why Mother Jones thought organizing labor unions was necessary.

3. How did Mother Jones and others go about organizing labor unions?

4. Determine why people like Mother Jones had so much difficulty creating and organizing the unions.

5. What conditions prompted Mother Jones to continue union organizing?

6. How does Mother Jones fit into the development of the union movement?

BACKGROUND/RESEARCH

COMMITMENT: the quality of making and keeping a pledge to follow a course of action or to support a policy or person.

Galileo

DATA:

Galileo (1564-1642) was a famous Italian astronomer, mathematician, and physicist. His work in the sciences included contributions in the field of mechanics—specifically acceleration, inertia, and motion—and in the field of astronomy—specifically in the arrangement of the planetary system and the development of the telescope. He also wrote papers on gravity and balance and developed the microscope, the thermometer, and the pendulum clock. Galileo found himself in a great struggle with the Roman Catholic Church. Because he advocated new ideas in opposition to ancient authorities like Aristotle, his work and writings were condemned by the Church. He questioned conservative beliefs and published work supporting the theories of Copernicus. Galileo was called to Rome and placed under house arrest. The Church demanded that he deny his beliefs. The issue Galileo pursued with vigor was the right of scientists to seek the truth. During his house arrest, he continued to carry on research, invent scientific instruments and write books which would lay the foundation for modern physics.

PROBLEM:

Design an argument for Galileo's defense against the popular beliefs of his day.

INVESTIGATIONS:

1. On what did Galileo base his beliefs?

2. Why was Galileo so committed to his beliefs?

3. How did Galileo's commitment result in his conflict with the Church? Explain.

4. Compare the beliefs of the Church with Galileo's beliefs.

5. How did Galileo's commitment to learning and knowledge extend beyond science into areas of the humanities?

6. What was the long-term effect of Galileo's commitment to his beliefs?

BACKGROUND/RESEARCH

COMMITMENT: the quality of making and keeping a pledge to follow a course of action or to support a policy or person.

Milo*

DATA:

Milo (Present Day...) is an unobservant, unmotivated boy who seems bored with his life. One day when he arrives home, he discovers a large, mysterious box in his room. The box contains an authentic tollbooth, traffic rules, a map, coins, and signs. Thinking that he has nothing better to do, Milo drives his toy car through the toll booth and begins a journey that takes him to strange new lands. On his journey he discovers the Kingdom of Wisdom, where the situation is very chaotic due to the loss of Rhyme and Reason. Milo learns that in order to save Rhyme and Reason, he must begin and complete a perilous mission of rescue. As a result of his commitment to the quest, Milo learns much about Wisdom, Knowledge, and himself.

*The Phantom Tollbooth, by Norton Juster

PROBLEM:

Write the next chapter of *The Phantom Tollbooth,* reflecting the effects of Milo's adventures and his commitment to Wisdom.

INVESTIGATIONS:

1. What causes Milo to make the commitment to rescue Rhyme and Reason?

2. What obstacles and difficulties does Milo face that challenge his commitment?

3. What lessons does Milo learn? Explain.

4. With whom does Milo ally himself? Why?

5. How does the quality of commitment change Milo?

6. What impact does Milo have on the characters he meets in Wisdom?

COMMITMENT: the quality of making and keeping a pledge to follow a course of action or to support a policy or person.

Cesar Chavez

DATA:

The son of a farm worker of Mexican descent, Cesar Chavez (1927-) organized a labor union for poor, itinerant Mexican-American farmworkers and became their spokesperson. He worked diligently for laws to protect farmworkers and to improve working conditions. Following the ideas of Mahatma Ghandi and Dr. Martin Luther King, Jr., Chavez strongly supported nonviolent action. Born in Arizona, he and his family became migrant workers in California when they lost their farm. In 1962 Chavez organized grape pickers in California and established the National Farm Workers Association. He organized successful boycotts of grapes and lettuce, and in 1973 his union evolved into the United Farm Workers of America. Despite great pressure, Cesar Chavez, personally committed to non-violence, said, ''The truest act of courage, the strongest act of manliness, is to sacrifice ourselves for others in a totally nonviolent struggle for justice.''

PROBLEM:

As Cesar Chavez, write a persuasive speech to be given to an angry group of workers encouraging them to commit themselves to a nonviolent approach to correcting injustices.

INVESTIGATIONS:

1. Research the history of the boycott.

2. What are nonviolent approaches to problem solving?

3. What impact have nonviolent approaches to problems had upon society?

4. How would Cesar Chavez define commitment?

5. Why were Martin Luther King, Jr., and Mahatma Ghandi role models for Cesar Chavez?

Commitment

COMMITMENT: the quality of making and keeping a pledge to follow a course of action or to support a policy or person.

IDENTIFY SOMEONE WHO EXEMPLIFIES COMMITMENT.
THE PERSON MAY BE FICTIONAL OR NON-FICTIONAL.

(name)

(graphic)

DATA:

PROBLEM:

INVESTIGATIONS:

1. What were the significant events of _____'s life?

2. Why were these events significant?

3. How might _____ have defined commitment? How would you define commitment?

4. Did _____'s response to the events of his/her life match his/her definition of commitment? Do they match yours?

5. How did _____'s response to events in his/her life demonstrate his/her commitment?

6. What event tested _____'s commitment the most? Why?

Commitment

COMMITMENT: the quality of making and keeping a pledge to follow a course of action or to support a policy or person.

USING YOURSELF, SHOW HOW YOU HAVE EXEMPLIFIED OR EXEMPLIFY COMMITMENT.

(your name)

(graphic)

DATA:

PROBLEM:

INVESTIGATIONS:

1. What significant event(s) of your life required you to commit to a cause?

2. Why were these events significant? Why did you commit?

3. Does your response to the events of your life match your definition of commitment?

4. How did your response to events in your life demonstrate your commitment?

5. What event tested your commitment the most?

GENEROSITY: the willingness to give; nobleness; largess.

Alfred Bernhard Nobel

DATA:

Alfred Nobel (1833-1896) was the Swedish chemist who invented dynamite and other explosives. His first successful detonation of dynamite occurred in 1862. Because of many accidents—including one which killed his youngest brother—Nobel was thought by many to be a public enemy. In 1867 he successfully changed the formula of dynamite and added a precision detonator which made the explosive safer to use. As a result of the success of his invention, Nobel became an extremely wealthy man. He believed, however, that his invention caused more death and destruction than good. His guilt led him to establish a large monetary fund—the bulk of his fortune—to reward work done for the betterment of mankind.

PROBLEM:

Judge the effect of Nobel's generosity against the effect of his invention.

INVESTIGATIONS:

1. How might Alfred Nobel define generosity? Explain.

2. How has his generosity affected mankind?

3. Why did Nobel invent dynamite?

4. How did Nobel intend dynamite to be used?

5. For which categories are the Nobel Prizes awarded? Why were these areas selected?

6. Did the establishment of the Nobel Prizes absolve the man of his guilt? Explain.

BACKGROUND/RESEARCH

GENEROSITY: the willingness to give; nobleness; largess.

Albert Schweitzer

DATA:

Born in France, Dr. Albert Schweitzer (1875-1965) was an extraordinary musician, clergyman, physician, missionary, theologian, writer, and philosopher. He was highly regarded in *all* of these fields! His entire life's work seems to have been based on a philosophy that he called ''reverence of life.'' In 1913 he left rewarding, comfortable and successful careers in Europe to open a clinic in Gabon (then French Equatorial Africa) at Lambrene. His selfless work began in a chicken coop but eventually led to the Nobel Prize in 1952. He used the $33,000.00 prize money to set up a leper colony and to expand the hospital at Lambrene. Dr. Schweitzer wrote many books. Among them was *The Philosophy of Civilization,* published from Africa in 1923. He traveled throughout the world, speaking and being honored for his work in Africa. Dr. Schweitzer devoted his entire professional life to the understanding of and appreciation for the dignity of human life.

PROBLEM:

Develop a plan and a set of reasons for establishing a Lambrene-type of mission somewhere in today's world.

INVESTIGATIONS:

1. Explain Schweitzer's ''reverence for life'' philosophy.

2. Why is the manner in which Dr. Schweitzer spent his life and talents unique?

3. What motivated Schweitzer to leave Europe for a life as a medical and religious missionary?

4. What successful careers did he leave when he left Europe?

5. What have been the results of his generosity?

6. How has Dr. Schweitzer's generous use of his life and skills been carried on after his death? Why?

BACKGROUND/RESEARCH

GENEROSITY: the willingness to give; nobleness; largess.

Josephine Baker

DATA:

Josephine Baker (1906-1975), famed black singer and dancer, was born in St. Louis, Missouri. She lived in one of the poorest sections of the city and at the age of eight she began working to support her family. When she was fourteen, she left St. Louis to live on her own in New York City; she got a job as a chorus dancer with the Dixie Steppers. By seventeen she was dancing in Noble Sissle's *Shuffle Along.* However, she soon left New York for Paris as a member of *La Negre,* an American jazz revue. She became an overnight success, gaining international fame. This led to a long and illustrious career on the stage and in film. In 1937 Ms. Baker became a naturalized French citizen. Throughout her life, she adopted orphaned children of many different races and nationalities. Her "rainbow tribe" consisted of twelve children. They lived with her in a castle in France. Also, because of her work with the French Resistance during World War II, she was awarded several medals, including the French Legion of Honor. Because of her generosity, she spent most of her fortune on her causes. She died in near poverty in Paris in 1975.

PROBLEM:

Create a movement composition that demonstrates Josephine Baker's concept of generosity.

INVESTIGATIONS:

1. What prompted Josephine Baker to create the "rainbow tribe"?

2. Why did Josephine Baker, an American, choose to live in France?

3. What did she do to be awarded the French Legion of Honor medal?

4. Why would her work for the French Resistance be considered a generous act?

5. How did the way in which Baker lived her life show her generosity?

6. What parts of Josephine Baker's early life influenced her to be a dancer and later to be so generous with her time and talent?

TRANSFER/APPLICATION

Generosity

GENEROSITY: the willingness to give; nobleness; largess.

IDENTIFY SOMEONE WHO EXEMPLIFIES GENEROSITY.
THE PERSON MAY BE FICTIONAL OR NON-FICTIONAL.

(name)

(graphic)

DATA:

PROBLEM:

INVESTIGATIONS:

1. What were the significant events of _____'s life?

2. Why were these events significant?

3. How might _____ have defined generosity? How would you define generosity?

4. Did _____'s response to the events of his/her life match his/her definition of generosity? Do they match yours?

5. How did _____'s response to events in his/her life demonstrate his/her generosity?

6. What event tested _____'s generosity the most? Why?

TRANSFER/APPLICATION

Generosity

GENEROSITY: the willingness to give; nobleness; largess.

USING YOURSELF, SHOW HOW YOU HAVE EXEMPLIFIED OR EXEMPLIFY GENEROSITY.

(your name)

(graphic)

DATA:

PROBLEM:

INVESTIGATIONS:

1. What significant event(s) of your life required you to be generous?

2. Why were these events significant? Why were you generous?

3. Does your response to the events of your life match your definition of generosity?

4. How did your response to events in your life demonstrate your generosity?

5. What event tested your generosity the most?

BACKGROUND/RESEARCH

RESPECT: the quality of being held in special regard; an act of giving attention; esteem; deference.

John Muir

DATA:

John Muir (1838-1914) was born in Dunbar, Scotland, to a farming family. At the age of eleven, his family moved to Wisconsin. There his love for nature took root. As a world traveler, Muir hiked throughout the United States, Europe, Asia, Africa, and the Arctic. The natural world was his classroom, where he studied ecology, botany, and biology. In 1892 he founded the Sierra Club, which has become a leading international organization for championing environmental concerns. As a result of his concerns for the preservation of nature, the destruction of the natural forests was monitored. However, Muir did not rest until legislation was passed by Congress guaranteeing protection of our natural treasures.

PROBLEM:

Evaluate the progress mankind has made concerning respect for the environment since John Muir's time.

INVESTIGATIONS:

1. As a result of Muir's efforts, what specific environmental sites were preserved?

2. What factors led to John Muir's respect for the natural environment?

3. What political influences did Muir use to help accomplish his goals for the environment?

4. What has been the impact of the Sierra Club on environmental awareness?

5. Why did it take so long for popular respect for the environment to match Muir's?

6. How and why does respect for the environment translate to conservation?

BACKGROUND/RESEARCH

RESPECT: the quality of being held in special regard; an act of giving attention; esteem; deference.

Eleanor Roosevelt

DATA:

Eleanor Roosevelt (1884-1962) was first known to the world as the wife of her fifth cousin, New York Governor and four-time elected United States President, Franklin Delano Roosevelt. As a child and young woman, she had been shy and withdrawn. After Franklin was stricken with polio in 1921, however, Eleanor traveled widely and spoke on his behalf to groups in Europe and Latin America as well as throughout the United States. In her travels she became aware of the plight of the poor and of minorities. As first lady—with the White House as her forum for weekly news conferences—she spoke out on issues related to the underprivileged and racial inequities. When her husband died in 1945, Eleanor at first felt that her life was over. In her 17 remaining years, however, she served as representative to the United Nations and chaired the Commission on Human Rights, which created the milestone UN Declaration of Human Rights. She also wrote a number of books and became a leader of behind-the-scenes activities of the Democratic Party. Throughout this latter part of her life, Eleanor continued to travel around the world, encouraging and supporting respect for the individual and for the disenfranchised and downtrodden among the world's people.

PROBLEM:

As Eleanor Roosevelt, write a proposal for a United Nations resolution which responds to a violation of the respect for human rights.

INVESTIGATIONS:

1. What specific things did Eleanor do in her life which gained her respect from the world community?

2. Of the programs/issues that Eleanor influenced, which best reflected her respect for the human condition?

3. How did Eleanor's travel on her husband's behalf influence her views on the human condition?

4. How did Eleanor's role as first lady influence future first ladies?

5. Why was Eleanor Roosevelt chosen to represent the United States in the United Nations?

6. How did Eleanor's respect for the presidency influence her marriage?

BACKGROUND/RESEARCH

RESPECT: the quality of being held in special regard; an act of giving attention; esteem; deference.

James (Jesse) Owens

DATA:

James (Jesse) Cleveland Owens (1913-1980) was an African-American track-and-field star. Born in Alabama, the son of a sharecropper, Jesse eventually attended Ohio State University and began breaking track records in competition. In 1936 Jesse Owens won four gold medals at the Summer Olympic Games in Berlin, Germany. He set Olympic records in the 200-meter race and the broad jump. Adolf Hitler, sure that German athletes would prove that Aryans were superior to other people, refused to congratulate or shake hands with Jesse Owens when he won the gold medals. Later, Owens went into the public relations business and traveled around the world giving speeches on fair play and patriotism. He believed that athletic competition could help solve political and racial problems. Respected around the world, Jesse Owens was described as "one of the best goodwill ambassadors" for the United States.

PROBLEM:

Write an editorial reacting to Hitler's treatment of Jesse Owens after his victory at the 1936 Olympics.

INVESTIGATIONS:

1. What characteristics did Jesse Owens exhibit that earned him respect beyond the athletic world?

2. Compare Jesse Owens to a contemporary sports figure.

3. How do the Olympic Games promote respect for people?

4. List contemporary figures who have characteristics similar to those of Jesse Owens. Why did you choose those people?

5. What is a job description for a "goodwill ambassador"?

61

TRANSFER/APPLICATION

Respect

RESPECT: the quality of being held in special regard; an act of giving attention; esteem; deference.

IDENTIFY SOMEONE WHO EXEMPLIFIES RESPECT. THE PERSON MAY BE FICTIONAL OR NON-FICTIONAL.

(name)

(graphic)

DATA:

PROBLEM:

INVESTIGATIONS:

1. What were the significant events of _____'s life?

2. Why were these events significant?

3. How might _____ have defined respect? How would you define respect?

4. Did _____'s response to the events of his/her life match his/her definition of respect? Do they match yours?

5. How did _____'s response to events in his/her life demonstrate his/her respect?

6. What event tested _____'s respect the most? Why?

Respect

RESPECT: the quality of being held in special regard; an act of giving attention; esteem; deference.

USING YOURSELF, SHOW HOW YOU HAVE EXEMPLIFIED OR EXEMPLIFY RESPECT.

(your name)

(graphic)

DATA:

PROBLEM:

INVESTIGATIONS:

1. What significant event(s) of your life required you to be respectful?

2. Why were these events significant? Why were you respectful?

3. Does your response to the events of your life match your definition of respect?

4. How did your response to events in your life demonstrate your respect?

5. What event tested your respect the most?

Bibliography

This is a selected general-use bibliography covering most of the personalities in *I Want to Be Like*. Specific bibliographic entries are available for individual personalities (biographies, autobiographies, trade books, historical references, etc.).

Adams, Russell L. *Great Negroes Past and Present*. Chicago: Afro-American Publishing Company, 1969.

Anderson, Jervis. *This Was Harlem*. New York: Farrar Straus Giroux, 1981.

Atkinson, Linda. *Mother Jones*. New York: Crown Publishers, Inc., 1978.

Bloom, Benjamin et al. *Taxonomy of Educational Objectives, Handbook 1: Cognitive Domain*. New York: David McKay Company, Inc., 1956.

McKay Company, Inc., 1956.

Children's Britannica. Chicago: Encyclopaedia Britannica, Inc., 1988.

Compton's Encyclopedia. F. E. Compton Co., 1984.

Encyclopaedia Brittanica. Chicago: Encyclopaedia Brittanica, Inc., 1980.

Faber, Doris. *Franklin Delano Roosevelt*. New York: Abelanrd—Schuman, 1975.

Hancock, Sibyl. *Famous Firsts of Black Americans*. Pelican Publishing Co., 1983.

Hogrogian, Robert. *Helen Keller*. Hawthorne, NJ: January Productions, Inc., 1981.

—. *Molly Pitcher*. Hawthorne, NJ: January Productions, Inc., 1979.

—. *Nathan Hale*. Hawthorne, NJ: January Productions, Inc., 1979.

—. *Sacajawea*. Hawthorne, NJ: January Productions, Inc., 1981.

—. *Thomas Alva Edison*. Hawthorne, NJ: January Productions, Inc., 1981.

Holmes, Edward and Christopher Maynard. *Great Men of Science*. New York: Warwick Press, 1979.

Juster, Norton. *The Phantom Tollbooth*. New York: Random House, 1961.

Low, Augustus N. and Virgil A. Clift (eds.). *Encyclopedia of Black America*. New York: De Capo Press, Inc. from McGraw-Hill, Inc., 1981.

Merit Student's Encyclopedia. New York: Macmillan Educational Corp., 1978.

McAlpine, Jim et al. *CPA: Be an Inventor*. New York: Sunburst Communications, 1983.

McAlpine, Jim et al. *CPS: Planning New Worlds*. New York: Sunburst Communications, 1982.

McAlpine, Jim et al. *What If?* San Luis Obispo: Dandy Lion Publications, 1985.

Montgomery, Lucy Maud. *Anne of Green Gables*. New York: Grosset & Dunlap, 1972.

New Book of Knowledge, The. Danbury, CT: Grolier, Inc., 1980.

O'Dell, Scott. *Island of the Blue Dolphins*. Boston: Houghton Mifflin, 1978.

Peare, Catherine Owens. *The FDR Story*. New York: Thomas C. Crowell Co., 1962.

Webster's Biographical Dictionary. Springfield, MA: G. and C. Mirriam Co., Publishers, 1971.

White, E.B. *Charlotte's Web*. New York: Harper & Row, 1952.

The World Book Encyclopedia. Chicago: Field Enterprises Educational Corp., 1986.